D. H. LAWRENC.  ꓳꓕES

D. H. Lawrence
IN 90 MINUTES

Paul Strathern

IVAN R. DEE
CHICAGO

D. H. LAWRENCE IN 90 MINUTES. Copyright © 2005 by
Paul Strathern. All rights reserved, including the right to
reproduce this book or portions thereof in any form. For
information, address: Ivan R. Dee, Publisher, 1332 North
Halsted Street, Chicago 60622. Manufactured in the United
States of America and printed on acid-free paper.

www.ivanrdee.com

Library of Congress Cataloging-in-Publication Data:
Strathern, Paul, 1940–
    D. H. Lawrence in 90 minutes / Paul Strathern.
        p. cm. —(Great writers in 90 minutes)
    Includes index.
    ISBN 1-56663-635-3 (cloth : alk. paper) —
    ISBN 1-56663-634-5 (pbk. : alk. paper)
    1. Lawrence, D. H. (David Herbert), 1885–1930.
    2. Authors, English—20th century—Biography. I. Title:
    D. H. Lawrence in ninety minutes. II. Title.

PR6023.A93Z92445 2005
823'.912—dc22
[B]
                                            2004056922

Contents

D. H. LAWRENCE IN 90 MINUTES

Introduction

By the end of his life, Lawrence had despaired of Western civilization, which he felt had corrupted and weakened the human spirit. He believed that we had somehow lost touch with our instinctual being and no longer responded to the "true voice" of our blood. We still possessed such truth deep within us, but it was smothered by a dead culture.

Three years before he died, Lawrence traveled in Italy and visited the Etruscan tombs. He became fascinated by this mysterious people which the Romans had "wiped out entirely in order to make room for Rome with a very big R." The Etruscans had vanished from their homeland, leaving little behind them. We could decipher their archaic Etruscan letters "that looked as if someone had just chalked them up yesterday without a thought. . . . But when we have read them we don't know what they mean . . . we cannot read one single sentence." Lawrence pondered this mysterious people and the fact that we now know nothing of them apart from what is left in their tombs.

So he goes to the tombs to see for himself. Here he is immediately struck that "One can live one's life, and read all the books [about the Etruscans] and never read a single word about the thing that impresses one in the first five minutes . . . that is, the phallic symbol." These symbols were all over the place, the entire site was littered with them. "Here it is, big and little, standing by the doors, or inserted, quite small, into the rock: the phallic stone!" Every man's tomb had one of these phallic stones. Lawrence speculated that their insistence upon these stones was the reason for the "annihilation of the Etruscan consciousness. . . . The new world wanted to rid itself of these fatal, dominant symbols of the old world, the old physical world."

Later he visits the tombs of Tarquinia: "the guide opens the iron gate, and we descend the steep steps down into the tomb. It seems a dark little hole underground: a dark little hole, after the sun of the upper world! . . . But the lamp flares bright, we get used to the change of light, and see. . . . It is very badly damaged, pieces of the wall have fallen away. . . . [Yet] as we take heart and look closer we see the little room is frescoed all round with hazy sky and sea, with birds flying and fishes leaping, and little men hunting, fishing, rowing in boats. . . . From the sea rises a tall rock, off which a naked man . . . is beautifully and cleanly diving into the sea. . . . Meanwhile a dolphin leaps behind . . . a flight of birds soars upwards to pass the rock, in the clear air. . . . It is all small and gay and quick with life, spontaneous as only young life can be. If only it were not so much damaged, one would be happy, because here is the real Etruscan liveliness and naturalness. It is not impressive or grand . . . just a sense of the quick ripple of life."

It is as if Lawrence were an Etruscan and had devoted his entire life to the quixotic attempt to resurrect a damaged culture enlivened by "the quick ripple of life." His works were an attempt to revive a life we have lost, and in them it is possible to glimpse something vivid, something now damaged, that we nonetheless recognize in ourselves. At his best, Lawrence reminds us of what we are, what it is we have lost. But it is a very tenuous argument, for all the vividness with which it is evoked. In Lawrence, deep sense often coexists with empty nonsense. The ranter coexisted with the prophet, just as his often dubious message coexisted with some of the finest writing in the English language. Lawrence had a genius for evocation, both of a past that may never in fact have existed, and of a luminous present that exists as never before in his words. This is his undeniable legacy.

The passage of Western civilization has been so overwhelming that we sometimes need to be reminded of what it has replaced. This requires a voice that recalls us to our origins—not to some redundant restrictive fundamentalism but to the joyous instinctual freedom we feel we may once have possessed. Lawrence was just such a voice.

Lawrence's Life and Works

David Herbert Lawrence was born in 1885 in the coal-mining village of Eastwood, which is set amidst the countryside five miles outside the industrial city of Nottingham, in the English midlands. He was the third son in a mining family, his closest brother Ernest having been born seven years earlier. His father was a charismatic figure, untamed by education and barely literate, who had gone down the pits at the age of ten. By all accounts he was a virile, intensely physical character, with bushy black hair and a heavy beard, who spoke in the thick local dialect. His mother, Lydia, had been a schoolteacher in the south of England and prided herself on a certain refinement. This refinement and her husband's forthright manner were, in their own different ways, to play a formative role in the temperament of their sons. Ernest was intelligent and athletic; the younger David Herbert always had a more frail physique but shared his brother's intelligence.

These qualities may have coexisted in the children but they made for conflict in the marriage. Lydia came from a strict churchgoing background and grew to despise her husband. She was determined that her children should "better themselves," and she soon became the dominant influence in the family, disparaging her husband in front of the children when he took to drinking. As a result, the children soon learned to shut their father out of their lives. Only many years later would Lawrence come to realize how much his mother's self-righteousness had cast a blight over both her husband and her children.

England at the time was a country riven by class and regional division as well as being smothered by sexual repression. Political power lay in the hands of an aristocratic country-house elite, and class distinction passed down through visibly stratified layers of a society where everyone was expected to "know their place." (Lawrence was born just two years after the death of Karl Marx in London.) Meanwhile a hypocritical press ensured that Victorian morality remained in place throughout all but the "lowest orders" of society, at the same time purveying sanitized (yet imagination-inspiring) accounts of the exploits of Jack the Ripper and the Oscar Wilde trial, both of which received sensational press coverage during Lawrence's childhood. And contrary to cherished historical myth, remarkably similar social conditions prevailed in the "civilized parts" of Europe and the Americas. For the most part, people behaved as they were expected to behave, or as they were told to behave. For those who wished to "get on in life," the prevailing ethos was conformity, especially to the behavior of one's "betters." Elocution lessons were popular among the aspiring lower middle class, into which Lawrence's mother had been born.

Lawrence's father, on the other hand, was proud of his heavy Nottinghamshire accent and dialect which was virtually incomprehensible to any outsider (geographical or social). After working all day down in the pit, deep under the earth in conditions hardly fit for an animal, he did not expect to behave like a civilized human being when he returned to the surface. Although ground down by the grimness and humiliation of his miner's life, he retained a remnant sense of freedom and belief in himself. Unlike so many of his countrymen, he sensed a way to behave that was true to his feelings. Eventually, coarsened by circumstance, he would lose sight of this; but his son would always retain this rare sense. And as Lawrence rose up the social scale, he would remain very much his own man. Despite all his acquired snobbery and arrogance, an integral part of his vision would always remain unblinkered. It would inspire one of his constant and central preoccupations: how is it possible to live one's life fully, without bowing to social pressure, while remaining in touch with one's deepest instincts and feelings. This was a lesson which many throughout the civilized Western world needed to learn. The young Freud, who was training as a psychiatrist in Vienna at this time, was not the only one to feel that in some unforeseen way civilization was beginning to warp human beings.

In 1898, at the age of thirteen, Lawrence won a scholarship to Nottingham High School. Three years later he left to begin work as a clerk in a local factory. Just as his mother had wished, he had escaped from the coarse mining culture of his father: he would not be condemned to work in the pit. Instead he had unwittingly escaped into a different form of oblivion. Here, as a clerk, he disappeared into the mass of similar semi-respectable lower-middle-class men grinding out their lives with no future. A life of pen-pushing and small-minded tedium was all that lay ahead for a clerk in the early twentieth century.

Such was the class of young men who would seize the opportunity to become "heroes" upon the outbreak of World World I, volunteering in the millions throughout Europe, only for their lives to be squandered amidst the squalor and slaughter of the trenches. World War I is often mistakenly assumed to have caused the breakup

11

of the old class-ridden order, which reigned supreme during this so-called Belle Epoque of European history. It was in fact merely a symptom, the outward manifestation of an inner decline: the social stagnation that characterized the early years of the twentieth century, when Lawrence was emerging from youth into early manhood. This stagnation, and its suffocating effects, would certainly have been felt, if not yet understood, by the young Lawrence in a dour provincial city such as Nottingham.

Yet elsewhere this was the period that saw the birth of modernism. Paris, Vienna, and even staid London were witnessing "the birth of the new." Futurism, cubism, psychoanalysis, the first airplanes, Einstein's relativity . . . so much implied that everything was going to change. Meanwhile, except among the intellectual few, nothing changed. And nothing might have changed for Lawrence had not disaster struck. His older brother Ernest, who had always been his mother's favorite, had gone to work in London at a shipping office. Then he took ill with pneumonia and suddenly died, leaving his mother distraught with grief. A few months later Lawrence himself was struck down with pneumonia and forced to leave his job. His mother nursed him through his illness, and while he recuperated at home she gradually transferred all her hopes and expectations to her next son.

The adolescent Lawrence at first reveled in this attention. It built his self-confidence no end, inspiring a belief in himself which he would always retain. Only later would he begin to realize how much his mother's love stifled him, subtly depriving him of the healthy independence he should have begun to develop at this period. At home convalescing, young Lawrence was encouraged to help his mother with household tasks. Donning an apron, he would help her make bread or potato cakes. In a mining village hidebound by tradition, such things were regarded as "women's work."

But he had also begun to read voraciously. After devouring the likes of Dickens, Shakespeare, Blake, and Shelley, he began searching out "modern" works in the local library. In this way he was soon absorbing Ibsen and Tolstoy as well as the scientific ideas of Darwin and the philosophy of Schopenhauer. Ideas, as well as literature, were a major inspiration from early on.

The Lawrence cottage was on the edge of the village; beyond the garden stretched the fields and woodlands of the open countryside. Lawrence became friendly with the Chambers family, who ran Haggs Farm, a couple of miles away across the fields. He was soon a regular visitor, helping out with jobs around the farm, bringing in the harvest with the family. He developed an easygoing closeness with the Chambers's eldest son Alan, but it was Alan's serious-minded sister Jessie who found herself most drawn to Lawrence. They soon developed an intense though largely intellectual relationship. Stimulated by his reading, Lawrence began to write poetry. In this he would express his feelings for Jessie, which she bewilderingly discouraged, though it was evident that she liked him. In one of his early poems, he describes her as:

. . . too chaste and pure
Ever to suffer love's wild attack.

By now Lawrence was working as a pupil-teacher in the local village school, a poorly paid position which involved trying to instill "the three r's" into miners' unruly children. In 1905 he took the exams for University College, Nottingham; and a year later, at the age of twenty-one, he entered the local university to study for a teacher's certificate. Jessie continued to encourage his writing, and between his studies he began writing stories as well as poems. Later he even began a novel. He also developed a talent for drawing and soon began painting as well. Jessie encouraged all these activities, but his mother was suspicious—both of what he was writing and of his friendship with Jessie. Lawrence, largely through the repressive influence of his mother, and Jessie, largely through her own natural temperament, both remained "fiercely virgin" (as he later put it). These repressive influences contributed to make Lawrence feel ashamed of the sexual feelings he now began experiencing.

In 1908 he graduated from college with his teacher's certificate and obtained a job at a school in Croydon, a southern suburb of London. He found teaching difficult, writing in a letter: "Think of a quivering greyhound set to mind a herd of pigs and you see me teaching." He clearly had a high opinion of himself and began cultivating a suitably genteel image so as to fit in at his middle-class lodgings.

Without telling Lawrence, Jessie sent some of his writing to Ford Madox Hueffer (later known as Ford Madox Ford), editor of the influential *English Review*. Hueffer was impressed and asked Lawrence to call at the magazine's office in central London. He soon befriended the somewhat gauche young schoolmaster from Croydon, publishing some of his stories and introducing him to a number of literary celebrities. In this way Lawrence met W. B. Yeats, whom he found an affected bore; H. G. Wells, then at the height of his fame, who struck Lawrence as "a funny little chap"; and Ezra Pound: "He is 24, like me—but his God is beauty, mine, life."

Lawrence had by this time completed his first novel, which had been rewritten several times with Jessie's guidance, and was now called *The*

White Peacock. He showed it to Hueffer, who declared, "It has every fault that the English novel can have," but added, "You've got genius." Hueffer passed it on to an influential editor, and it was accepted for publication.

The White Peacock was very much a first novel, with much thinly disguised autobiography. It contained much that was expected of a novel during this period, and no small amount of social affectation. Yet it also contained, in embryo, many themes and some of the characters that Lawrence would rework in his masterpieces. Most noticeably, it displays something of the best and worst of his ability to characterize other human beings in his own searching emotional terms:

> She quivers with feeling; emotion conquers and carries havoc through her, for she has not strong intellect, nor a heart of light humor; her nature is brooding and defenseless; she knows herself powerless in the tumult of her feelings, and adds to her misfortunes a profound mistrust of herself.

But most telling of all is his description of the feelings that Cyril has for his friend George, which develop as they bring in the harvest together. This amounts to a superb evocation of early love. Cyril is Lawrence himself, and George is based upon Jessie's brother Alan. Together they go swimming, and afterward, as George dries himself, Cyril cannot help but gaze in wonder at "the noble, white fruitfulness of his form." In a deeply revealing passage, which also reveals the "genius" noticed by Hueffer, Lawrence describes how

> He saw I had forgotten to continue my rubbing, and laughing he took hold of me and began to rub me briskly as if I were a child, or rather, a woman he loved and did not fear. I left myself quite limply in his hands. And, to get a better grip of me, he put his arm around me and pressed me against him, and the sweetness of the touch of our naked bodies against each other was superb. It satisfied in some measure the vague, indecipherable yearning of my soul, and it was the same with him. When he had rubbed me all warm, he let

go, and we looked at each other with eyes of still laughter, and our love was perfect for a moment, more perfect than any love I have known since, either for man or woman.

Lawrence would of course later become famous (and notorious) for his celebration of heterosexual lovemaking. Many have claimed that this passage demonstrates his homosexuality, or at least his bisexuality. Such ingredients may well have formed a constituent element of his psyche, but it must be remembered that at this period he was still an unhealthily repressed virgin. For all the talk of charged feelings between people in the novel, in life he was sexually undeveloped. In this aspect at least, he remained in his adolescence, where sexual feelings can be both intense and intensely repressed, to the extent that they are not yet fully focused on the opposite sex. As a description of such feelings, this passage from *The White Peacock* achieves a dreamlike libidinous veracity. What Lawrence described certainly happened, as did his feelings, but sex at this stage remained for him a dream.

A year or so after he came to teach in London, Lawrence eventually broke off his relationship with Jessie. He became briefly engaged to a fellow schoolteacher, to whom he appears to have lost his virginity, though not the disgust at sex which he seems to have picked up from both Jessie and his mother.

By now Lawrence's mother was dying of cancer, and he was able to place a copy of his first published novel in her hands shortly before she died. It is doubtful whether she managed to read the book. In this aspect at least, his father's reception of the book was identical. He tried the first page but was unable to decipher it.

"And what did they gi'e thee for this, lad?" he asked.

"Fifty pounds, Father."

"Fifty pounds! An' tha's never done a day's work in thy life!"

Lawrence was devastated by his mother's death. He continued writing but with little of his previous force or direction. Then he suffered another bout of pneumonia. Emerging from a period of emotional and physical turmoil, he found himself able to set down for the first time what he really wanted to say. He began writing a novel about his relationship with his mother, which would eventually become his first full-length masterwork, *Sons and Lovers*.

The plot of the novel is heavily autobiographical, and little attempt is made to disguise this. It is set in the Nottinghamshire mining village of Bestwood. The hero is a young painter called Paul Morel. His father, Walter, is a rough and ready miner; his mother is a woman who comes from a middle-class family fallen on hard times. She has had a strict Christian upbringing and has a powerful character. She becomes disillusioned with her marriage and comes to invest all her hopes in Paul. He develops a relationship with the bookish Miriam, of whom his mother disapproves. The relationship is blighted by his mother's possessiveness. In a departure from autobiography, Paul then has a relationship with Clara Dawes, a factory worker with independent ideas who is separated from her husband.

They make love together, but this is somehow not enough.

> He felt more and more that his experience had been impersonal, and not Clara. He loved her. There was a big tenderness, as after a strong emotion they had known together; but it was not she who would keep his soul steady. He had wanted her to be something she could not be.

The possessiveness of Paul's mother and its undermining effect on her son's relationships with women has been characterized as a deeply perceptive description of Freudian depth psychology. Freud had recently identified the Oedipus complex, so called after the Greek tragic hero who unwittingly married his mother. It was Freud's contention that all sons unconsciously do battle with their father in the attempt to gain the love of their mother—though Lawrence's version was in fact more concerned with a mother's love of her son.

Lawrence apparently did not know Freud's work when he began *Sons and Lovers*, but he became acquainted with it while he was writing the novel. Fortunately it did not affect his writing; Lawrence had a deep belief in himself which could not be deflected by someone else's theory, even when it might appear to "explain" what he was writing. He would certainly have recognized the blatant truth of Freud's idea, but his novel was an evocation of an Oedipus complex as it was experienced, the subtle nuances of its effects as they were played out upon a mother and her son. This was the truth that Lawrence knew, rather than the findings of any depth psychology. No such intellectual knowledge could deflect him from the knowledge gained by means of his "intelligent heart"; Lawrence's powers were essentially intuitive and instinctive. In *Sons and Lovers* he does not theorize about psychology so much as live it. Yet this lived (rather than cogitated, or constructed) experience, which he set down so convincingly and accurately on the page, was not devoid of its own knowledge. Lawrence the writer was deeply aware of what was happening between Paul and his mother, and subtly suggested its psychological effects as their relationship unfolded in the novel. This may have been his autobiography lived out on the page, but in the writing of it Lawrence became self-aware, and the authorial presence covertly points the reader toward such awareness and understanding.

Yet to do this involved Lawrence in such daring self-exposure that most would have flinched from its honesty. In one scene Paul returns, having taken Miriam home, to find his mother sitting in her rocking chair. She chides him about Miriam and his apparent absorbtion in her, until Paul is goaded to tell his mother: "No, mother—I don't really love her. I talk to her, but I want to come home to you." Paul takes off his collar and tie, and rises "bare-throated," ready to go to bed.

As he stopped to kiss his mother, she threw her arms around his neck, hid her face on his shoulder, and cried, in a whimpering voice, so unlike her own that he writhed in agony:

"I can't bear it. I could let another woman—but not her. She'd leave me no room, not a bit of room—"

And immediately he hated Miriam bitterly.

"And I've never—you know, Paul—I've never had a husband—not really—"

He stroked his mother's hair, and his mouth was on her throat.

"And she exults in taking you from me—she's not like ordinary girls."

"Well, I don't love her, mother," he murmured, bowing his head and hiding his eyes on her shoulder in misery. His mother kissed him, a long fervent kiss.

"My boy!" she said, in a voice trembling with passionate love.

Writing of such experience with integrity, without the protection of irony or any other distancing device, requires intense self-belief to carry it off. The conversations in *Sons and Lovers* are filled with honest words which cover deep inarticulate or oblique feelings. The characters are aware, yet not aware; and the author is seldom knowing—more, he is absorbed so much in the writing that his creeping understanding must become our growing understanding. There is little room for dissent; we either swallow Lawrence whole or fling the book away—in disgust, derision, or self-protection. Life need not be like this: Lawrence insists that it is.

Sons and Lovers ends with Paul Morel getting into a fight with Clara Dawes's husband, and then his mother dying. In this way he is released. Yet the loss of his mother all but destroys him. On the final page Paul cries out to his dead mother as he walks along the street at night:

> She was the only thing that held him up, himself, amid all this. And she was gone, intermingled herself. He wanted her to touch him, have him alongside with her.
>
> But no, he would not give in. Turning sharply, he walked towards the city's gold phosphorescence. His fists were shut, his mouth set fast. He would not take that direction, to the darkness, to follow her. He walked towards the faintly humming, glowing town, quickly.

As a result of Lawrence's bout of pneumonia, he was not able to go back to teaching immediately. He made a life-changing decision: from now on he would live by his writing. This was a brave choice for a virtually unknown and barely published young author. At the time he was still some way from completing *Sons and Lovers*. After a number of unsatisfactory, unconsummated affairs in London, he returned to Eastwood. Here he soon began having cold feet about giving up teaching. He dreamt up the idea that maybe he could obtain a position teaching English at a small German university. Hoping to obtain a letter of introduction, he approached his old French teacher at Nottingham University, Professor Weekley, and was invited to lunch.

Here Lawrence met the professor's aristocratic German wife, Frieda, who was a member of the von Richthofen family (which also produced the "Red Baron," the celebrated World War I fighter ace). Frieda had been brought up in the family castle and was nominally a baroness. She was also tall, blonde, and described by several people who met her as "a magnificent Brunhilde." The mother of three children, she was bored with life in provincial England. On her regular trips "to visit her family" she mingled among high society and intellectuals in Berlin, having the odd passing affair with one celebrated figure or another before returning home to family life in Nottingham.

Lawrence had met a number of famous writers and upper-class hostesses in London. Though prone to snobbishness, he had tried hard not to be dazzled, judging them for the most part as bourgeois in attitude and distinctly lacking in any working-class vigor. But he had never before encountered an aristocrat like the thirty-two-year-old Frieda.

Lawrence was now twenty-six: a tall, thin, gangling young man with flaming red hair and moustache. Yet all who met him attest to something exceptional about him, something that marked him out—a quality that sometimes caused street urchins to jeer at him. There was a distinctly primitive quality in him—the echo of his writing, which belied his puny form. When Frieda first saw him, "He seemed so obviously simple. Yet he arrested my attention. There was something more than met the eye. What kind of a bird was this?"

Lawrence was incorrigibly intense, and as such incapable of polite small talk. When he encountered Frieda, he immediately launched into a passionate denunciation of women, explaining how he was no longer interested in getting to know them. Frieda was intrigued by this approach. Despite what he said, it soon became clear that he was intrigued by her. She appeared not in the least interested in her husband, he noticed. Lawrence and Frieda continued to talk through lunch, through the afternoon, until finally it was dark. In an elated state, Lawrence took his leave and walked eight miles through the night across the fields to his home. He soon plucked up the courage to write her a letter, in which he declared, "You are the most beautiful woman in all England." And how many women in England do you know? she responded wryly when they met a few days later. It became evident that Lawrence had fallen in love with her.

Frieda was even more intrigued. When her husband was away, she suggested that Lawrence spend the night with her. But Lawrence was outraged at this suggestion. There was always an element of prudishness in him, and he was anything but casual by nature. He had no interest in embarking upon a casual affair, he explained to her. For him, Frieda was "the woman of a lifetime." He demanded that she inform her husband and go away with him. Something about Lawrence made Frieda realize that she loved him as well. Things quickly snowballed, and within a few weeks she took her children to London, leaving them with their English grandparents. On May 3, 1912, she met Lawrence at Charing Cross Station, and together they eloped on the Channel ferry to the Continent. Lawrence had first set eyes on Frieda only six weeks earlier and was now leaving England with just eleven pounds in his pocket. He and Frieda sat on the deck watching England sink into the grey sea like an "ash-grey coffin."

Lawrence had staked his life—something he took intensely seriously—on a aristocratic married woman he scarcely knew. And in her own fashion Frieda had staked everything on this gauche but stangely compelling writer chap. It had not been easy for her to abandon her children, but in the end she had been swept off her feet—as much as he himself had been swept off his feet. In this mutually bewildered state they traveled to the German border town of Metz to stay with Frieda's family.

Lawrence's first night with Frieda was not a success—both were carrying too much emotional baggage. The emotional turmoil had stirred up in Lawrence all manner of guilty feelings about his mother, Jessie, his failed affairs, and much else. Frieda, for her part, was tormented with guilt at abandoning her children, at leaving her husband so abruptly. In a poem of remarkable honesty, Lawrence evokes what happened:

> In the darkness
>> with the pale dawn seething at the
>>> window
>> through the black frame
>> I could not be free,
>> not free myself from the past, those
>>> others—

and our love was a confusion,
there was a horror,
you recoiled away fom me.

Yet things quickly settled down, to the point where Lawrence could write:

> I know in my heart "here's my marriage."
> . . . It's a funny thing to feel one's passion—sex desire—no longer a sort of wandering thing, but steady, and calm. I think, when one loves, one's very sex passion becomes calm, a sort of steady force, instead of a storm. Passion, that nearly drives one mad, is far away from real love.

During those first hectic days, Lawrence and Frieda tentatively got to know each other. In the words of Lawrence's biographer Jeffrey Meyers: "Frieda was an attractive mixture of good and bad qualities. Spontaneous, generous, and passionate, she was also indolent, selfish, and amoral." By the time they traveled south to Italy at the end of the summer for a belated "honeymoon," Frieda had already been unfaithful to Lawrence on more than one occasion. In a way, she was still uncertain about him. She confessed to him what she had done, perhaps more to see what would happen than out of honesty. Far from being devastated, Lawrence forgave her. Perceptively, he understood her need for freedom; he knew he would never win her by attempting to tame her, an attempt at which her husband had so evidently failed. Years later the writer Aldous Huxley, who knew them both well, wrote with insight about their relationship:

> Frieda and Lawrence had, undoubtedly, a profound and passionate love-life. But this did not prevent Frieda from having, every now and then, affairs with Prussian cavalry officers and Italian peasants, whom she loved for a season without in any way detracting from her love for Lawrence or from her intense devotion to his genius. Lawrence, for his part, was aware of these erotic excursions, got angry about them sometimes, but never made the least effort to break away

from her; he realized his own organic dependence upon her.

Lawrence needed Frieda, but he also sought to dominate her, after his own fashion. He saw the relationship between man and woman as a conflict, which the man must eventually win. His attempts to gain Frieda's "submission" would last all his life, making for a long and stormy but indestructibly close relationship. She, for her part, had never been so loved, so needed. With Lawrence, she was not just the woman in a man's life, she was Woman herself. She responded with her "devotion to his genius," encouraging his already heady self-belief and his insistence upon a domination he would never achieve. All this would generate sufficient material for Lawrence's essentially autobiographical imagination to last him a lifetime.

In a villa on the shore of Lake Guarda in northern Italy, Lawrence completed the final draft of *Sons and Lovers*, which would be published the following year in 1913, gaining him a measure of the recognition he so craved and deserved. He now embarked upon a period of extreme creativity. Of this time he wrote, "This is the best I have known or ever shall know." He was happily in love as well as writing prose, poems, and even plays. He now started into *Twighlight in Italy*, which marked his entry into what was for him a new genre—travel writing. The opportunity for lyrical flights, for precise but poetic evocation of landscape, places, and people, and above all the opportunity to express himself on whatever passing notion took his fancy—all this was a godsend to Lawrence, giving him the freedom to express himself as never before. As a result, his travel writing contains flashes of both the best and the very worst of Lawrence. He describes himself sitting writing in a deserted lemon garden high on the hillside above the lake. He evokes the winter sunlight, "so still and pure, liked iced wine," and the advent of almond and apricot blossom at springtime "like pink puffs of smoke among the grey smoke of olive leaves." But this is no idyll. The timeless pagan world of peasant life was disappearing forever as the Italians surrendered to the modern world, emigrating to the factories of northern Europe, to America, where "this great mechanized society, being self-less, is pitiless. It works on mechanically and destroys us, it is our master and our God." Lawrence's feeling for the gods, both modern and ancient, was profound:

> I went into the church. It was very dark and impregnated with centuries of incense. It affected me like the lair of some enormous creature. My senses were roused, they sprang awake in the hot, spiced darkness. My skin was expectatant, as if it expected some contact, some embrace. . . . It was a thick, fierce darkness of the senses. But my soul shrank.

At around this time he also wrote, in a letter: "My great religion is a belief in the blood, the flesh, as being wiser than the intellect. We can go wrong in our mind. But what our blood feels and believes and says, is always true." Only superficially does this credo appear more profound than Lawrence's preceding description of entering the dark church. In the church he is feeling in words, in the credo he is reducing his feelings to words. The former speaks volumes; the latter is, in the last analysis, all but empty of meaning other than as an anti-intellectual stance. Admittedly the mind can lead us astray—especially when its ratiocinations take insufficient account of our needs as sentient beings, the primitives from which we have evolved. But what precisely does it mean to say that "the blood [is] wiser than the intellect"? What precisely is it that "our blood feels and believes and says" that is "*always* true." The key word here is "precisely." The noble, primitive, and instinctual feelings that Lawrence wishes to promote as our only wisdom become dangerous nonsense when they are seen as "always true." Our instincts are not always correct, or beneficial, or even tolerable. Correctional institutions are filled with instinctive characters, detained for the good of themselves and society.

Essentially Lawrence's credo, as expressed here, is an individual poetic emotion. We feel we know what he is saying, but only in the most general sense. In this context it is worth comparing

Lawrence's words here with that other famous poetic credo, Keats's:

> "Beauty is truth, truth beauty"—that is all
> Ye know on Earth, and all ye need to know.

Again, viewed literally (prosaically, if you like), this is of course nonsense. Viewed poetically, as an individual response to the world, it can be seen as heroic, romantic, spiritually inspiring, or simply reckless. Yet it achieves its force by being stated as a universal principle. Try rendering it: "For me, something that is beautiful is true. . . . This is all I feel I need to know." Likewise, Lawrence's credo: "What I call the voice of my blood . . . always speaks the truth for me." But where Keats's credo served for the most part as a guiding principle which covertly inspired his poetry, Lawrence's credo would show an increasing tendency to take over his work. In its most literal appearances, it would be a disaster. When it merely informed his outlook, it would result in many challenging insights as well the genius for understanding people that can make his writing so exceptional. When, in the years to come,

Lawrence wrote as the man who entered the "spiced darkness" of the church where his "soul shrank," he would achieve greatness. When he expanded on his credo, often descending into empty bullying, his art suffered. He had discovered what drove his vision. In doing so, Lawrence the writer had given birth to Lawrence the preacher, and through the years to come they would make awkward bedfellows.

The same phrase could be used to describe Lawrence and Frieda. Temperamentally, and in so many other ways, they were polar opposites. Put simply, they believed in living their lives differently and had no real wish to do otherwise. Frieda was aristocratic, used to being waited on by servants, and believed in enjoying herself. She liked lying in bed, reading novels, smoking, with little care for what others thought of her. Lawrence remained to a certain extent working class in his attitudes. He was industrious, conscientious, and in many ways retained the puritan outlook on life he had inherited from his mother. As a result, he would work all day writing, then do the housework and cooking that Frieda considered beneath her. Yet he did not seem to mind doing all this. In the rather harsh judgment of Huxley's wife: "Frieda is silly. She is like a child, but he likes her *because* she is a child."

By now Frieda was trying unsuccessfully to obtain a divorce from Professor Weekley, and she had begun to miss her children terribly. In the summer of 1913 she and Lawrence had a violent row, which ended with her breaking a plate over his head—apparently the first, but certainly far from the last occasion on which this would happen. She then ran off, leaving Lawrence bruised and bemused. Two days later she returned, and Lawrence agreed to travel with her back to England.

In May 1914, Frieda at last managed to obtain a divorce, and she married Lawrence at the Kensington registry office in west London. By now Lawrence was well into a novel called *The Sisters*. The first part of this would eventually became a novel in its own right, called *The Rainbow*.

The Rainbow begins as a pastoral family saga, telling the story of the Brangwens, who live at Marsh Farm beside the river Erewash on the border of Nottinghamshire. Initially the Brangwens are totally absorbed by their work, with the seasons passing in almost mythical fashion:

> In autumn the partridges whirred up, birds in flocks blew like spray across the fallow, rooks appeared on the grey, watery heavens, and flew cawing into the winter. Then the men sat by the fire in the house . . . and the limbs and the body of the men were impregnated with the day, cattle and earth and vegetation and the sky, the men sat by the fire and their brains were inert, as their blood flowed heavy with the accumulation from the living day.

Gradually this pastoral idyll is invaded by the modern world. Coal mines appear farther up the river valley, and in 1840 a canal is constructed across the meadows. The Brangwen family too, start to change, emerging as characters and beginning to take on individualistic consciousness. Yet at the same time, the price for this independence seems to be a gradual separation of heart and mind. These individuals are no longer so at ease with themselves.

Eventually we come to the third generation (whose life span parallels Lawrence's own) and are introduced to Ursula Brangwen, who is the focus of the last third of the book. Ursula emerges as very much a "modern woman" (of her period), who is aware that "to be oneself was a supreme, gleaming triumph." She grows up having a loving but difficult relationship with her father. Like Lawrence, she becomes a pupil-teacher and then goes to university. More than any of the predecessors in her family, she feels the gap between her emotions and her intellect.

Ursula's journey to self-discovery involves an exploration of her sexuality. She finds herself attracted to the soldier Anton Skrebensky and begins an affair with him. Their sexual encounter is described in explicit detail, but Lawrence's aim is far from titillation. It is his attempt to show the vital struggle between man and woman at first-hand in its most crucial act. Eventually we become aware of Skrebensky's softness, his weakness, his inadequacy when confronted with a "real" woman. In the end, he is too conventional: he represents all that is staid and ordinary in Britain and the empire in which he is a soldier. His inability to achieve any meaningful contact with Ursula in the end renders him impotent in the face of her passion.

In another development, while Skrebensky is away serving in South Africa, Ursula embarks upon an experimental lesbian affair with "her mistress" Winifred Inger. "Their lives seemed suddenly to fuse into one, inseparable." Winifred helps Ursula to develop, sharing with her all she knows. "They took religion and rid it of its dogmas, its falsehoods. Winifred humanized it all. Gradually it dawned upon Ursula that all the religion she knew was but a particular clothing to a human aspiration. The aspiration was the real thing. . . ." Lawrence recounts in some detail how Ursula lies "in her mistress's arms, her forehead against the beloved, maddening breast." This does not lead to fulfillment, however, and later Ursula becomes aware that only "a heavy, clogged sense of deadness began to gather upon her, from the other woman's contact."

At the close of the novel, Ursula is left alone. "She was the naked, clear kernel thrusting forth the clear powerful shoot, and the world was a bygone winter, discarded." She stands watching a rainbow, God's biblical promise to the world. "She saw in the rainbow the earth's new architecture, the old, brittle corruption of houses and factories swept away, the world built up in a living fabric of Truth, fitting to the overarching heaven."

By now World War I had broken out. Lawrence was opposed to the war for a variety of reasons, not the least being that he was married to a German. This led him to a deeper understanding of the faults on both sides. Although he was in many ways aggressive by temperament, he became a pacifist, declaring: "Kill a man by order that has never done me any harm? No, I couldn't do it. They can kill me first." As news of the senseless carnage in the trenches of Flanders reached England, Lawrence became increasingly despondent about the war and its effects.

The success of *Sons and Lovers* had given Lawrence and Frieda access to upper-class intellectual society, most notably to the Bloomsbury Group. Along with members of the group he was invited by Lady Ottoline Morrel for weekends at Garsington, her Elizabethan country house set amidst delightful gardens and the Oxfordshire countryside. Here Lawrence met Bertrand Russell, Virginia Woolf, and Lytton Strachey, as well as several other well-known academics and intellectuals. The snob in Lawrence was proud to be hobnobbing with such sophisticated types; the intense working-class puritan in him could not help despising many of them as shallow socialites. Lawrence's increasing renown bolstered his self-confidence. His superb insight enabled him to link what he saw and experienced on these country weekends to the larger historical events taking place:

> So much beauty and pathos of old things passing away and no new things coming: this house of Ottoline's—it is England—my God, it breaks my soul—this England, these shafted windows, the elm-trees, the blue distance— the past, the great past, crumbling down,

breaking down, not under the force of the coming buds, but under the weight of many exhausted, lovely yellow leaves, that drift over the lawn and over the pond, like the soldiers, passing away, into winter and the darkness of winter—no, I can't bear it.

Lawrence struck up an intense friendship with Bertrand Russell, who was at the time Lady Ottoline's lover. Russell was also widely regarded as the leading philosopher in Europe. Furthermore, he was a pacifist and involved in a public campaign against the war (which would later result in him being sent to prison). Lawrence and Russell were drawn together as opposites, each seeing in the other something he lacked. As a result of his close friendship with Russell, Lawrence found himself drawn to articulate his inchoate intellectual ideas, which were inspired by emotion rather than reason. He declared himself against democracy, which he saw as the cause of contemporary society's ills. Russell, who was a great champion of democracy, was horrified. Undeterred, Lawrence then contradicted himself by outlining the kind of democracy *he* believed in:

> I don't want tryrants. But I don't believe in democratic control. . . . The thing must culminate in one real head, as every organic thing must—no foolish republics, with foolish presidents, but an elected King, something like Julius Caesar. . . . There must be an elected aristocracy.

Inevitably Lawrence's deep friendship with Russell would end in an equally deep quarrel. In the course of this, Russell claimed to see in Lawrence the irrational impulses that had led to the war. Lawrence, for his part, claimed to see in Russell the lack of feeling and defects of character which, repeated on the larger stage, had in his view been responsible for the war. The effect of this on Lawrence was catastrophic, at least in the short term. He began trying to work out his psychological ideas, trying to set them down as "philosophy," as distinct from letting them inspire his fictional writing. These ideas culminated

in much stirring nonsense, all the more dangerous for being stirring:

> We have actually to go back to our own un-
> conscious. But not to the unconscious which
> is the inverse reflection of our ideal con-
> sciousness. We must discover, if we can, the
> true unconscious, where our life bubbles up
> in us, prior to any mentality. The first bub-
> bling life in us, which is innocent of any al-
> teration, this is the unconscious. It is pristine,
> not in any way ideal. It is the spontaneous
> origin from which it behooves us to live.

This is little better than "a belief in the blood
[which] is always true." A close two-year friendship with the finest intellect in the land had re-
sulted only in Lawrence's "blood" being
transformed into equally irrational psychological
jargon.

For Lawrence, the only answer now was to
abandon civilization altogether and set up a
utopian society. This would become for him
more than a mere dream. His utopia was to be
called Rananim—from the Hebrew words in

Psalm 23, *ranenu rananim*, meaning "Rejoice in the Lord, O ye Righteous." Rananim would be peopled by like-minded friends who sought to escape the collapse of civilization. Lawrence's utopian delusion (to call it a scheme would be to lend it a practicality that it never possessed) would persist for several years, its intended location changing from an orange grove in Florida to a Greek island, or a South Sea island, or the eastern slopes of the Andes. (Curiously, though Lawrence would spend the rest of his life traveling the world, often ending up in extremely remote destinations, he would in fact visit none of these places.) At any rate, his aim was:

> I want to gather together about twenty souls and sail away from this world of war and squalor and found a little colony where there shall be no money but a sort of communism as far as necessaries of life go, and some real decency. It is to be a colony built up on the real decency which is in each member of the Community—a community which is established upon the assumption of

goodness in the members, instead of the assumption of badness.

How this "assumption of goodness" was to be reconciled with everyone acting according to their "pristine . . . spontaneous . . . unconscious" remained unclear, such legislation being set out only in a jumble of poetic generalizations. But it is too easy to mock. Indeed, in a major writer such a lapse, or mental hobbyhorse, would perhaps be best forgotten—were it not for the fact that such ideas remained very much a central part of Lawrence's life and works. They were always there, frequently informing some of his finest writing. This is an object lesson for us all. Such wrongheaded ideas do not necessarily invalidate the imagination they inspire. As Lawrence himself understood only too well, some of our finest thoughts have a dark origin. . . . But back to utopia. One by one, Lawrence's closer friends, such as Russell, were invited to join the "twenty souls" destined for Rananim; and one by one, like Russell, they were struck off the list with biblical finality. Only Lawrence, and a seemingly insouciant Frieda, remained permanently on the list.

In 1915 *The Rainbow* was published. Although Lawrence's publisher optimistically declared that the novel would "blaze a path into the future," the critics thought otherwise and chose to judge it by the straitlaced standards of the past. One critic judged the story of Ursula Brangwen's journey to self-realization to be "a monstrous wilderness of phallicism," another saw it as "an orgy of sexiness." Within weeks the courts had declared *The Rainbow* obscene and ordered all copies of the novel to be destroyed. Lady Ottoline Morrell's husband was persuaded to raise the matter in Parliament, but to no avail. Lawrence was close to despair. He soon found himself virtually penniless, living in a remote cottage on the Cornish coast, under suspicion of being a German spy because of Frieda. He quarreled with a succession of friends, breaking off with them in bitter letters, his turbulent emotions bringing him to the brink of insanity. In the end he did the only thing that could ever save him: he sat down and began writing a novel. It derived from the second half of his projected novel *The Sisters*, and was in many ways a sequel to *The Rainbow*. It was called *Women in Love* and would prove to be his finest work, containing much of the best, and not a little of the worst, of his genius.

In *Women in Love* Lawrence examines once more the whys and wherefores of human relationships—man and woman, as well as man and man. The opening of the novel finds the sisters Ursula and Gudrun Brangwen (from *The Rainbow*) teaching in the grammar school at Beldover, a midland mining town. The bones of the story are simple enough. Ursula falls in love with the school inspector Rupert Birkin (a very thinly disguised portrait of Lawrence himself). Gudrun, the young art teacher, finds herself attracted to Birkin's friend Gerald Crich, whose father owns the local mine. The novel follows the development of these two relationships as well as that between Birkin and Crich. Lawrence manages, through Birkin, to deliver himself of his opinions on how people should try to live and how they should attempt to relate to one another. Lawrence was well aware of this hectoring tendency in Birkin, and self-deprecatingly describes his manner as that of "a Sunday-school teacher, a prig of the stiffest type." Despite this self-awareness, Lawrence-Birkin persists in preaching on all and sundry throughout the novel. But at the same time he is searching out the possibilities of some form of "real" existence amidst the sophistication and commercialization of the modern world.

Initially Birkin is involved in a somewhat un-satisfactory affair with the neurotic and eccentric Hermione Roddice, a cutting portrait of Lady Ottoline Morrell. His growing relationship with Ursula Brangwen involves both attraction and repulsion. Lawrence casts all reticence to the wind in his attempts to divine how man and woman should live together. Birkin's self-analysis is both anguished and daringly self-revealing:

> He knew his life rested with her. But he would rather not live than accept the love she proffered. The old way of love seemed a dreadful bondage, a sort of conscription.

What it was in him he did not know, but the thought of love, marriage and children, and a life lived together, in the horrible privacy of connubial satisfaction, was repulsive. He wanted something clearer, more open, cooler, as it were. The hot narrow intimacy between man and wife was abhorrent.

Birkin's struggle for self-fulfillment reaches beyond the circumstances of the life he finds himself living, and he is determined to follow his thoughts wherever they are led by his feelings.

On the whole, he hated sex, it was such a limitation. It was sex that turned a man into the broken half of a couple, the woman into the other broken half. And he wanted to be single in himself . . . he wanted a further conjunction, where man had being and women had being, two pure beings, each constituting the freedom of the other, balancing each other like two poles of one force, like two angels, or two demons.

Interspersed with such musings are some passages of pure Lawrence, when he simply allows his genius to shine through. In one passage Gerald Crich is out riding and encounters Ursula and Gudrun Brangwen in a country lane on their way back from school, as they wait for the train to pass at the closed gate of a level crossing: "Whilst the two girls waited, Gerald Crich trotted up on a red Arab mare. He rode well and softly, pleased with the delicate quivering of the creature between his knees. . . . He was well-set and easy, his face with its warm tan showed up his whitish, coarse moustache." The approaching locomotive, "with the sharp blasts of the chuffing engine," suddenly frightens Gerald's horse. "The mare rebounded like a drop of water from hot iron." Terrified, Ursula and Gudrun press themselves back into the hedge as Gerald "sat glistening and obstinate, forcing the wheeling mare, which spun and swerved like a wind, and yet could not get out of the grasp of his will." As the train passes, "The mare opened her mouth and rose slowly, as if lifted on a wind of terror. Then suddenly her fore feet struck out, as she convulsed herself utterly away from the horror. Back she went, and the two girls clung to each other, feeling she must fall backwards on top of him." Gerald forces the mare round. "She roared as she breathed, her nostrils were two, wide, hot holes, her mouth was apart, her eyes frenzied. It was a repulsive sight. But he held on her unrelaxed, with an almost mechanical restlessness, keen as a sword pressing in to her. Yet he seemed calm as a ray of cold sunshine."

Birkin's attempt to form a deep and intense relationship with Gerald eventually results in one of the most vivid and meaningful scenes in the book. Gerald is at home, standing before the fire in the library, suffering from "an agony of inertia," desperate for something to save him "from the misery of nothingness, relieve the stress of this hollowness." On cue, Birkin arrives. "When he saw Birkin his face lit up in a sudden, wonderful smile." They fall into conversation, and Birkin soon persuades Gerald that the answer to their close but slightly awkward relationship is for them to wrestle naked together on the carpet in front of the fire.

So the two men began to struggle together. They were very dissimilar. Birkin was tall and narrow, his bones were very thin and fine. Gerald was much heavier and more plastic. His bones were strong and round, his limbs were rounded, all his contours were beautifully and fully molded. . . . [Birkin] impinged invisibly upon the other man, scarcely seeming to touch him, like a garment, and then suddenly piercing in a tense fine grip, that seemed to penetrate into the very quick of Gerald's being.

They then stop to discuss "methods," such as "practiced grips" and "throws"; and after this it's back to the fray:

So the two men entwined and wrestled with each other, working nearer and nearer. . . . [Birkin] seemed to penetrate into Gerald's more solid, more diffuse bulk, to interfuse his body through the body of the other . . . playing upon the limbs and trunk of Gerald like some hard wind. It was as if Birkin's whole physical intelligence interpenetrated into Gerald's body, as if his fine, sublimated energy entered into the flesh of the fuller man. . . .

And so on. . . . The reason I have quoted this passage at some length is because this seems simultaneously to contain both the finest and the most ludicrous in Lawrence. I say seems—because which is which? Lawrence was far too good a writer not to know what he was doing. He would not inadvertently have made a fool of himself in such a fashion. In fact, it is worth considering precisely what he seriously thought he was trying to do. (He reckoned he could ignore the cheap sniggers.)

In this passage Lawrence is both metaphorical and utterly literal, *at the same time*. Birkin is certainly struggling for a greater intimacy with Gerald in their real life, and their struggle certainly contains a metaphorical homosexual element that repeatedly threatens to spill over into literalness. But the fact is, it does not. In his own real life, Lawrence's homosexuality was repressed; and in the book Birkin-Lawrence's wrestling partner was seemingly not a homosexual, repressed or otherwise. Much of the force of this scene lies in its many ambiguities. Lawrence was attempting to show—metaphorically as well as literally—that it was possible for us to try to get to know each other better, that deep friendship should also include an aspect of intimate physical familiarity. This was, in many ways, his project for personal relationships, for civilization even—or at least for his utopia. We should be more open, more close, more emotionally comfortable with each other—and for this to happen there is a required physical element.

Once upon a time we had been easier and more intimate with one another, but this personal familiarity had been lost with the advance of civilization. Here Lawrence may well be right; but his attempt to recapture this, to reimpose it upon human relationships, seems to have been utterly doomed. It may have been possible for us to behave like this in our peasant past, but it is neither possible nor necessary now in our modern world. Or is it? Lawrence's project has failed as an everyday occurrence. We simply do not behave in such a manner. On the other hand, since Lawrence's time we have learned to live much more easily with our emotions, our sensuality, and our differing sexualities. Lawrence would make an interesting distinction here. He was all for sexuality but against sensuality, the latter being far too decadent and relaxed for him. Our modern easygoing attitude to our sexuality would also have horrified him. As far as he was concerned, this was all a very serious business—as indeed it is when we first come to terms with our sexuality. And here Lawrence still has much to say. His artistic genius invests such matters with a sacredness that we are all capable of experiencing to begin with. Perhaps inevitably, when we advance beyond this adolescent stage, or beyond the first intensity of love, our life becomes less hormone-driven as we direct our energies elsewhere. For the most part, we lose the intensity that Lawrence would have us retain.

Yet Lawrence's project, in its more intense and ecstatic aspect, cannot be said to have vanished altogether. It is certainly visible when we see teams of males celebrating a goal or a victory. And this intimacy is very public; indeed, that is part of it—it is a celebration. In light of this, Lawrence's attempt is not entirely risible. Just as it is not entirely driven by his repressed homosexuality. We can attain this state, but it seems we cannot live this way—not on a permanent basis. Life is just not like that, certainly not for intelligent civilized individuals who have progressed beyond the tribal stage.

From the vantage point of Lawrence's time and place—the heart of the world's largest empire during World War I—it may well have looked as if something had gone very wrong with the way people behaved toward one another. Public outrage could be roused by the description of a young woman attempting to explore her sexuality, to discover her authentic intuitional and primitive self—as a result, *The Rainbow* was banned. Yet at the same time young men in their thousands were being sacrificed in the trenches in a manner reminiscent of the vast primitive human sacrifices that caused the steps of Aztec temples to become waterfalls of blood. Modern civilization had not lost its primitivism, it had merely dehumanized it.

By the beginning of the twenty-first century we have progressed beyond such anomalies, or so we like to think. Lawrence must be credited with having attempted to identify the root of such peculiarities, and having attempted to find a solution. In his time, few were willing to attempt such a task, few even recognized (or were willing to admit) that anything was wrong. For this we remain in Lawrence's debt. Just because our solution is so very different from the one he envisaged does not mean that we have nothing to learn from his diagnosis of our existential ills. Our quest to discover ways of living with the primitive self out of which we have evolved remain with us. We do not have to live the way we find ourselves living. Indeed, one thing is certain in this aspect of our history: there is a great difference between the way we ourselves have chosen to live, compared with the repressed and difficult way people lived with themselves in Lawrence's time. We have left behind this past in order to attempt a different, more rational and scientific way of living. But this difference is likely to be as nothing compared to the difference between our way of living and that chosen by people in the next century. And this transformation will lead us into an as yet unimaginable scientific world. The coming advances of genetics, evolutionary psychology, and even social understanding will change utterly our conception of what we are. In Lawrence's time, such questions of self-conception were for the most part not even being asked. Society, the mores by which we lived, and thus our self-conception, were all but set in stone. Lawrence was, in many ways, a pioneer in provoking us to ask such questions about ourselves. In this at least, we still need his example.

After World War I, Lawrence and Frieda left England. Apart from fleeting visits, they would never live there again. In 1919 they settled in Italy. Lawrence had now grown the famous red beard, the virile growth behind which he would shelter for the rest of his life. His philosophical ideas had now developed to the point where he saw himself as the prophet of a new religion. This was prompted by his feeling that "Vitally, the human race is dying. It is like a great uprooted tree, with its roots in the air. We must plant ourselves again in the universe." Such feelings were commonplace in the aftermath of World War I. There was a widespread longing for change, for an overthrowing of the old order that had led to such a catastrophe. This feeling had already led to widespread social unrest, most notably in the Russian Revolution. But Lawrence's remedy was not political or even revolutionary. It was, if anything, conservative—though in a characteristically Lawrentian sense. In his view, our entire civilization was wrong.

I honestly think that the great pagan world of which Egypt and Greece were the last living terms, the great pagan world which preceded our own era once, had a vast and perhaps perfect science of its own, a science in terms of life. In our era this science crumbled into magic and charlatanry.

64

Lawrence's ultimate aim was to establish nothing less than a new form of consciousness—one which was more in touch with our intuitive living being. Obviously this could not be done overnight, and it could not be done in the midst of the modern civilization that had robbed us of so much of our original pagan selves.

Lawrence still had hopes for leading his utopian project. Partly in order to prepare for setting up Rananim, he now began writing down his ideas in a work called *Fantasia of the Unconscious*. This contains his thoughts on how we can connect with "the great science previous to ours" which he believed was "established all over the then-existing globe . . . was esoteric [and] invested in a large priesthood." Such intuition is just credible, if highly questionable; but alas this was only the starting point. What follows is a wild ragbag of biblical exhortation ("To your tents, O Israel!"), psychological gibberish ("the root of conscious vision is almost entirely in the breast"), and scientific error ("Mr. Einstein's Theory of Relativity does not supersede the Newtonian Law of Gravity"). Its proposals are nonsense ("Let no child learn to read, unless it learns by itself, and of its own individual persistent desire").

Toward the end of this short work, Lawrence appeared to be working toward his idea of leadership:

> But when once a woman *does* believe in her man, in the pioneer which he is, the pioneer who goes on ahead beyond her, into the darkness in front, and who may be lost for ever in this darkness . . . How wonderful it is to come back to her, at evening, as she sits half in fear and waits!

The topic of leadership was developed somewhat more prosaically in the novel he now began writing, *Aaron's Rod*. The story is set in the dark of wartime London and the bright southern sun of Italy. It is filled with much ill-digested autobiographical material and contains thinly disguised portraits of people Lawrence met in Italy. The novel involves two men, Aaron and Lilly. Aaron abandons his wife and children on Christmas Eve "because I'm damned if I want to go on being a lover, to her or anybody." Having left his job as a coal-miner, he finds work as a flutist in a London orchestra. Lilly, on the other hand, is a natural leader among men, who maintains his separateness from others and impresses his authority without arrogance. In the sadly perceptive words of Lawrence's biographer Jeffrey Meyers: "Aaron expresses Lawrence's fear of dominating women and longing for a man; Lilly is Lawrence's female self longing for a male." This element comes to the fore in an extraordinary scene where Lilly gives the naked Aaron's body a long and loving massage, during which he "rubbed it all warm and glowing with camphorated oil, every bit of it." It is difficult to look upon this novel as much more than a fantasized attempt by Lawrence to work out his sexual ambiguities. In the end, the problem remains unresolved. Aaron finds himself unable to allow himself to love a man, yet refuses to live with a woman. At the end, Lawrence returns to an old theme: "Freak and outsider as he was, Lilly *knew*. He knew, and his soul was against the whole world."

On such evidence it is easy to consider that Lawrence, for all his great imaginative talent, had simply lost it. Fortunately, this was not the case. He was always a prodigious worker, and at the same time he was writing his *Fantasia*, and an even greater fantasy in the form of his novel, he continued to express his true genius in short stories, poems, and travel writing. Indicatively, such forms do not readily accommodate hectoring philosophy or fantasized sexual self-analysis. While such topics are not entirely absent in this domain of Lawrence's output, they are at least held to a minimum.

Lawrence's travel book *Sea and Sardinia* dates from this period. Here his descriptive writing is as vivid as ever, and is given even greater depth by a knowledge of his historical credo:

Cold, fresh wind, a blue-black, translucent rolling sea on which the wake rose in a snapping foam, and Sicily on the left. . . . These coasts of Sicily are very imposing, terrific, fortifying the interior. And again one gets the feeling that age has worn them bare: as if old,

old civilizations had worn away and exhausted the soil, leaving a terrifying blankness of rock.

Lawrence is often accused of humorlessness. This is not strictly true, as a vein of sardonic humor pervades much of his disgust at modern civilization and his description of the types which it throws up. This is hardly the stuff of laughter, though—it is more a jeering which spills over from his intensity and contempt. Yet when Lawrence was more relaxed, he was quite capable of being genuinely funny, at least on occasion. In *Sea and Sardinia* he recounts an episode when he is traveling on a bus through the remote hinterland. The bus stops to let on a man who is carrying "two little black pigs, each of which is wrapped in a little sack, with its face and ears appearing like a flower from a wrapped bouquet." The bus driver insists that before the new passenger can travel, he must also pay a fare for "each pig as if it were a Christian." An altercation breaks out, and "the little pigs open their black mouths and squeal with self-conscious appreciation of the excitement they are causing." The driver insists that "every animal, even if it were a mouse, must be paid for." Whereupon one of his passengers drily remarks: "How much do you charge for the fleas you carry?" Eventually, speechless with anger, the man returns to his mule and reties his pigs on either side of the saddle on its back. Meanwhile the pigs, "looking abroad from their new situation, squeal the eternal pig-protest against an insufferable humanity."

Lawrence was particularly good at describing animals, with which he seemed to find a deep empathy. For him, they were in many ways more in tune with their "natural being" than many of us modern human beings. The pagan condition to which Lawrence wished us to return had many animal affinities, especially in its reliance on "the truth of the blood" and "animal intelligence." Despite any covert agenda, Lawrence remains as true as he can to the animals he describes. His evocations are seldom sentimental and seldom overly brutal: they have their own dignity. This said, his animal poetry achieves a masterly ambiguity of intense realism and metaphor. His poetic evocations of animals succeed in being both powerfully animaline and emblematic of a human element. Take for instance his poem "The Baby Tortoise." The subject is introduced as "a tiny, fragile, half-animate bean," and Lawrence remarks how "no one ever heard you complain" at being amidst the "vast inanimate" of the world. "What a huge vast inanimate it is that you must row against." Lawrence asks:

> Do you wonder at the world as you slowly
>   turn your head in its wimple
> And look with laconic, black eyes?
> Or is it sleep coming over you again,
> The non-life?

As Lawrence once wrote in a letter about his poetry: "I have always tried to get an emotion out in its own course, without altering it. It needs the finest instinct imaginable, much finer than the skill of the craftsmen. . . . I don't write for your ear. . . . I can't tell what *pattern* I see in any poetry, save one complete thing." At his best, in both prose and poetry, Lawrence achieves even more than this. As in his late poem "Shadows":

> And if tonight my soul may find her peace
> in sleep, and sink in good oblivion,
> and in the morning wake like a new-opened
> flower
> then I have been dipped again in God, and
> new-created.

Such was the consciousness for which Lawrence strove—and in himself, on many occasions, achieved. It was, if anything, his attempt to legislate for such an ineffable state that led him astray. He wanted us all "dipped again in God," striving for this as an enduring condition of being. While all of us can recognize such a state, with appropriate wonder, not all of us wish to spend our lives in pursuit of such an essentially poetic vision. Civilization may have crippled the pagan in us, but it has its consolations, even if these do often fall short of the ecstatic consciousness prescribed by Lawrence. And modern civilization is far from devoid of its own epiphanies—from the personal to the social, from the abstract reverie of scientific discovery to the tribal clamor of witnessing the winning touchdown. We are not entirely devoid of intensity of being. It is just that our experience in this sphere tends to be neither pagan (in the specific manner that Lawrence would wish it) nor to have overtly ancient roots. We can wonder at a film of the earth taken from space, or at a distant galaxy photographed by the Hubble telescope, just as much as our primordial naked vision of the starlit heavens.

In 1922, Lawrence and Frieda decided to travel to America. While writing a work of criticism, *Studies in Classic American Literature*, he had concluded that the American West was the uncorrupted haven of natural living that he had been searching for. The Lawrences chose to travel to America by the eastern route, calling for a brief stay with friends in Ceylon (now Sri Lanka), before arriving in Australia. There they spent over three months, most of it in the coastal village of Thirroul, fifty miles from Sydney. They lived an isolated life in the village, walking along the beach and swimming. Despite living in a cottage called "Wyewurk," Lawrence completed a novel about Australia, called *Kangaroo*, in just six weeks. This work is chiefly of interest for its autobiographical revelations concerning the persecution Lawrence suffered during World War I in England, because of his pacifist views. According to Lawrence's views expressed in *Kangaroo*, this treatment was responsible for his rejection of society. The novel also examines his attitudes toward socialism and the growing idea of fascism, both of which he eventually rejects.

In August 1922 the Lawrences set sail across the Pacific for America, where they eventually took up the invitation of the wealthy Mabel Dodge Sterne, a patron of the arts, to live on her estate at remote Taos, near Santa Fe in New Mexico. According to Lawrence: "The moment I saw the brilliant, proud morning shine high up over the deserts of Santa Fe, something stood still in my soul, and I started to attend." Despite Lawrence's difficult relationship with Mabel Sterne, she continued to be generous to the Lawrences. The Lawrences now had little money, and his health was in an increasingly frail state.

The illness that weakened his lungs had by now been diagnosed as tuberculosis, though he refused to acknowledge it. Frieda continued chain-smoking, and they both continued coughing and arguing together in their habitual, companionable manner. The warm dry climate was deemed good for Lawrence's health; he became interested in local Indian and Mexican culture; and he soon returned to artistic activities. He began composing some superb poems, painting pictures, and above all writing prose. As ever, he quickly marshaled his ideas into a novel, which would become *The Plumed Serpent*. Read from a purely political view, this work has distinctly fascist implications; but Lawrence was in fact attempting to explicate something far deeper than any mere political tyranny based upon spurious racial theories. He now felt that the only way civilization could redeem itself was by abandoning Christianity and democracy, which only sapped the vital energy and primitive strengths of humanity. Instead each region of the world should revive its own ancient religion. *The Plumed Serpent* features a prophet-hero, the Mexican general Don

75

Ramon Carrasco. He attempts to revive the ancient Aztec religion of Quetzalcoatl, whose leaders were regarded as gods by the people. Instead of liberal egalitarianism, Carrasco wishes for an authoritarian theocracy with almost mystical powers, under which the people will rediscover the instinctual vision of their blood. These distressing, dangerous, and for the most part balmy ideas are as ever accompanied by some superb writing. Lawrence's descriptive and evocative prose seemed particularly attuned to Mexico.

> Everything going vague in the immense sunshine, as the air invisibly thickened, and Kate could feel the electricity pressing like hot iron on the back of her head. It stupefied her like morphine. Meanwhile the clouds rose like white trees from behind the mountains, as the afternoon swooned in silence, rose and spread black branches, quickly, in the sky, from which the lightning stabbed like birds.
>
> And in the midst of the siesta stupor, the sudden round bolts of thunder, and the crash and the chill of rain.

This union of prose and place was even more evident in the travel book he wrote at this time, *Mornings in Mexico*:

> Nowhere more than in Mexico does human life become isolated, external to its surroundings, and cut off tinily from the environment. Even as you come across the plain to a big city like Guadalajara, and see the twin towers of the cathedral peering around in the loneliness . . . your heart gives a clutch, feeling the pathos, the isolated tininess of human effort. As for building a church with one tower only, it is unthinkable. There must be two towers, to keep each other company in this wilderness world.

Lawrence pushed himself hard, too hard for a man of his physique, and on the very day he wrote the last words of *The Plumed Serpent* he suffered a bronchial hemorrhage. This was brought on by a combination of malaria (which he had picked up in Ceylon) and typhoid (from Mexico) attacking his already weak lungs. The result was a resurgence of what was unmistakably tuberculosis. It now became evident that Lawrence was very ill, and he returned to Europe. After a brief stay in England, he settled in Italy, near Florence, in 1926. Here he began writing the novel which would, decades later, turn him into a household name: *Lady Chatterley's Lover*, the most explicitly sexual of all his works. In it he would describe how sexuality expressed itself in love, reinforcing his message by the use of explicit sexual descriptions and explicit sexual language.

Lady Chatterley's Lover describes the relationship that forms between Connie (Lady Chatterley) and Mellors, the gamekeeper on her estate. Mellors is clearly based on Lawrence himself, just as Lady Chatterley bears a close resemblance to Frieda when she and Lawrence first met. Lawrence proclaimed that in this work he wanted to evoke "the warm blood-sex that establishes the living and revitalizing connection between man and woman." Connie's encounter with the primitive sexuality of Mellors brings about a renewal of her entire being. The intensity of their sexual relationship breaks down all class barriers by the "democracy of touch."

In the short summer night she learnt so much. She would have thought a woman would have died of shame. Instead of which, the shame died. Shame, which is fear: the deep organic shame, the old, old physical fear which crouches in the bodily roots of us, and can only be chased away by the sensual fire, at last it was roused up and routed by the phallic hunt of the man, and she came to the very heart of the jungle of herself. She felt, now, she had come to the real bedrock of her nature, and was essentially shameless. She was her sensual self, naked and unashamed. She felt a triumph, almost a vainglory. So! That was how it was! That was life! That was how one self really was!

It is necessary to read the book to understand precisely how Connie reaches this ecstatic state, and to realize precisely the act she is describing.

Lawrence also intended his novel to illustrate what was wrong with class-ossified England, what indeed was crippling all civilized humanity. He makes this clear from the dramatic opening

words: "Our is essentially a tragic age, so we re-
fuse to take it tragically. The cataclysm has happened, we are among the ruins." Yet he insists:
"We have got to live, no matter how many skies
have fallen."

Lawrence was soon made aware that his attempt to describe sex openly and honestly, to
give it an intense and sacramental quality free
from all prudish restraint, would find no publisher in Britain. So in 1928 he decided to risk
having it published privately in Florence, at his
own expense. The book was hand-printed and
cost £300 (around £3,000, or $2,000, at today's
prices). But the gamble paid off, despite the book
being quickly banned in Britain and America.
Aided by friends willing to smuggle copies,
Lawrence more than managed to recover the ini-
tial outlay which he could barely afford.

By 1929 it was clear that Lawrence was dying. He briefly visited England where an ex-
hibiton of his paintings was raided by the police
because of their frank, colorful, and joyful por-
trayal of male nudity. Eventually he settled at
Vence in the South of France, where he wrote

Apocalypse. This is Lawrence's commentary on the last book in the Bible, the Book of Revelations. It shows, if there had ever been any doubt about it, the essentially religious motivation which lay behind Lawrence's ideas. But it remained very much his own religion:

> What man most passionately wants is his living wholeness and his living unison, not his own isolate salvation of his "soul." Man wants his physical fulfillment first and foremost, since now, once and only, he is in the flesh and potent. For man, as for flower and beast and bird, the supreme triumph is to be most vividly, most perfectly alive.

In the end Lawrence came to see himself more as a prophet than as a writer. Fortunately, for all his hectoring insistence upon the renewal of our instinctual being, his instinctual abilities as a writer continued to shine through, and to the end he was capable of writing lines of transcendent simplicity and lucidity:

> Now it is autumn and the falling fruit
> and the long journey towards oblivion.

81

The apples falling like great drops of dew
to bruise themselves an exit from
    themselves.

And it is time to go, to bid farewell
to one's own self, and find an exit
from the fallen self.

In 1930, at the age of just forty-four,
Lawrence died in the sanatorium at Vence. Five
years later his ashes were taken to Taos, where
they were placed by Frieda in a small shrine to
his memory, which stands on the mountainside
above the valley of the Rio Grande.

Afterword

In the year that the unknown D. H. Lawrence met and eloped with Frieda von Richthofen Weekley, he declared boldly: "I think the new generation is rather different from the old. I think they will read me more gratefully." It would take almost thirty years for this prophecy to come true.

During the decades immediately following his death, Lawrence's ideas about "blood-truth" appeared uncomfortably close to many similarly entitled Nazi ideas. As a result, his image became tarnished. This was not entirely unjust. Lawrence's ideas were certainly elitist, but not on Nazi racial grounds; much of his preaching loosely used terms that were open to a wider interpretation than he intended. But there can be no doubt whatsoever that Lawrence himself would have been horrified and disgusted at Nazi doctrines. Had he lived, he would certainly have distanced himself from such nonsense.

By the 1950s, Lawrence had begun to attract a measure of the literary acclaim he deserved. In particular he was championed by the renowned but controversial English literary critic F. R. Leavis, who had been inspired by Lawrence to believe that literature was something more than high cultural entertainment. The life-enhancing properties of Lawrence's work had great effect on a generation of graduates from Cambridge, where Leavis taught. Still, his novels attracted little attention beyond the literary sphere.

Thirty years after Lawrence's death, this situation would change dramatically. In 1959 in America, and in 1960 in Britain, Lawrence's publishers decided to contest the ban on *Lady Chatterley's Lover*. The resulting court cases showed how much "the new generation is rather different from the old." Lawrence's prophesy had come true, and the gap between the generations had now opened into a chasm. The British lawyer for the prosecution made the revealing remark that *Lady Chatterley's Lover* was "not the sort of book you would want your servants to read." Such sentiments belonged to an irrevocable past; some of the children of these servants were now lawyers themselves. Meanwhile, leading literary figures stood in line to defend the novel and its qualities. The publishers won on both sides of the Atlantic, and in Britain alone three million copies of *Lady Chatterley's Lover* sold in the following six months. The permissive 1960s had begun.

Lawrence himself would of course have been outraged by the era of sexual liberty, but his newly released work played a crucial role in the moral transformation that followed. Arguably, no other literary work has ever had so much effect. There can be little doubt that part of Lawrence's wish had come true, and that a new generation would indeed "read him more gratefully."

It is easy to overlook this historic aspect of Lawrence's work. It is just as easy to deride his often ludicrous ideas. Yet there is more to Lawrence than these aspects. Two major qualities of his work remain as relevant today as they were when he was alive. The evocative, instinctual genius of his writing remains as rare and as fresh as ever. Few in the entire history of literature can match him here. Second, his intuitive insights into the male-female relationship also remain utterly relevant. In an age of political correctness and female emancipation, many of his views will certainly appear sexist. Yet it is worth remembering that he was also hard on men who fell short of his demanding standards. His insights into the war between the sexes still reads with all the veracity of a frontline observer. In this war he was no pacifist: instead he insisted upon being a constant, unflagging, and convinced combatant. He wanted to win, but he grudgingly had to admit that he knew what it was like to lose. And he knew his enemy: Frieda was no mean adversary! At the same time Lawrence's ambivalent sexuality made him aware of many nuances that might have eluded a less sensitive participatant. His insights into how and why we win and lose in this war are still relevant to the ongoing conflict.

From Lawrence's Writings

This piece is taken from a Lawrence short story called "The Fox." The two women, March and Banford, run Bailey Farm together, and need to protect their chickens:

The fox really exasperated them both. As soon as they had let the fowls out, in the early summer mornings, they had to take their guns and keep guard; and then again, as soon as evening began to mellow, they must go once more. And he was so sly. He slid along in the deep grass, he was difficult as a serpent to see. And he seemed to circumvent the girls deliberately. Once or twice March had caught sight of the white tip of his brush, or the ruddy shadow of him in the deep grass, and she had let fire at him. But he made no account of this.

One summer evening March was standing with her back to the sunset, her gun under her arm, her hair pushed under her cap. She was half-watching, half-musing. It was her constant state. Her eyes were keen and observant, but her inner mind took no notice of what she saw. She was always lapsing into this odd, rapt state, her mouth rather screwed up. It was a question whether she was there, actually consciously present, or not.

The trees on the wood-edge were a darkish, brownish green in the full light—for it was the end of August. Beyond, the naked, copper-like shafts and limbs of the pine-trees shone in the air. Nearer, the rough grass, with its long, brownish stalks all agleam, was full of light. The fowls were round about—the ducks were still swimming on the pond under the pine-trees. March looked at it all, saw it all, and did not see it. She heard Banford speaking to the fowls, in the distance—and she did not hear. What was she thinking about? Heaven knows. Her consciousness was, as it were, held back.

She lowered her eyes and suddenly saw the fox. He was looking up at her. His chin was pressed down, and his eyes were looking up. They met her eyes. And he knew her. She was spellbound—she knew he knew her. So he looked into her eyes, and her soul failed her. He knew her, he was not daunted.

She struggled, confusedly she came to herself, and saw him making off, with slow leaps over some fallen boughs, slow, impudent jumps. Then he glanced over his shoulder, and ran smoothly away. She saw his brush held smooth like a feather, she saw his white buttocks twinkle. And he was gone, softly, soft as the wind.

She put her gun to her shoulder, but even then pursed her mouth, knowing it was nonsense to pretend to fire. . . .

From a wartime letter written to Lady Ottoline Morrell in February 1915, in which Lawrence ponders the future:

After the War, the soul of the people will be so maimed and so injured that it is horrible to think of. And this shall be the new hope: that there shall be a life wherein the struggle shall not be for money or for power, but for individual freedom and common effort towards good. That is surely the richest thing to have now—the feeling that one is working, that one is part of a great, good effort or of a great effort towards goodness. It is no good plastering and tinkering with this community. Every strong soul must put off its connection with this society, its vanity and chiefly its fear, and go naked with its fellows, weaponless, armorless, without shield or spear, but only with naked hands and open eyes. Not self-sacrifice, but fulfillment, the flesh and the spirit in league together, not in arms against one another. And each man shall know that he is part of the greater body, each man shall submit that his own soul is not supreme even to himself. "To be or not to be" is no longer the question. The question now is how shall we fulfill our declaration, "God is." For all our life is now based on the assumption that God is not—or except on rare occasions. . . . We must go very, very carefully at first. The great serpent to destroy is the will to Power, the desire for one man to have some dominion over his fellow-men. Let us have *no* personal influence, if possible—nor personal magnetism, as they used to call it, nor persuasion—no "Follow me"—but only "Behold." And a man shall not come to save his own soul. Let his soul go to hell. He shall come because he knows that his own soul is not the be-all and end-all, but that all souls of all things do but compose the body of God, and that God indeed shall *Be*.

A passage from Sea and Sardinia, *where Lawrence describes an actor in a village play. Is it an example of his supreme insight into his fellow human beings—or, alternatively, his need to impose his ideas upon all people he encountered? In fact, as so often with Lawrence, it appears as a beguiling mixture of both.*

It was this contradiction within the man that made the play so interesting. A robust, vigorous man of thirty-eight, flaunting and florid as a rather successful Italian can be, there was yet a secret sickness which oppressed him. But it was no taint in the blood, it was rather a kind of debility in the soul. That which he wanted and would have, the sensual excitement, in his soul he did not want it, no, not at all. And yet he must act from his physical desires, his physical will.

His true being, his real self, was impotent. In his soul he was dependent, forlorn. He was childish and dependent on the mother. To hear him say, "Grazia, mamma!" would have tormented the mother-soul in any woman living. Such a child crying in the night! And for what?

For he was hot-blooded, healthy, almost in his prime, and free as a man can be in his circumstances. He had his own way, he admitted no thwarting. He governed his circumstances pretty much, coming to our village with his little company, playing the plays he chose himself. And yet, that which he would have he did not vitally want, it was only a sort of inflamed obstinacy that made him so insistent, in the masculine way. He was not going to be governed by women, he was not going to be dictated to in the least by any one. And this because he was beaten by his own flesh.

His real man's soul, the soul that goes forth and builds up a new world out of the void, was ineffectual. It could only revert to the senses. His divinity was the phallic divinity. The other male divinity, which is the spirit that fulfils in the world the new germ of an idea, this was denied and obscured in him, unused. And it was this spirit which cried out helplessly in him through the insistent, inflammable flesh. Even this play-acting was a form of gratification for him, it had in it neither real mind nor spirit.

The passage from Women in Love *where Ursula walks into the night, looking for she knew not what, at the same time feeling that "The more one could find a pure loneliness, with no taint of people, the better one felt":*

She started, noticing something on her right hand, between the trunks. It was like a great presence, watching her, dodging her. She started violently. It was only the moon, risen through the thin trees. But it seemed so mysterious, with its white light and deathly smile. And there was no avoiding it . . . she turned off along the hill-side. . . . The moon was transcendent over the bare, open space, she suffered from being exposed to it. There was a glimmer of nightly rabbits across the ground. The night was as clear as crystal, and very still. She could hear a distant coughing of a sheep.

So she swerved down to the steep, tree-hidden bank above the pond, where the alders twisted their roots. She was glad to pass into the shade out of the moon. There she stood, at the top of the fallen-away bank, her hand on the rough trunk of the tree, looking at the water, that was perfect in the stillness, floating the moon upon it. But for some reason she disliked it. It did not give her anything. She listened for the hoarse rustle of the sluice. And she wished for something else out of the night, she wanted another night, not this moon-brilliant hardness. She could feel her soul crying out in her, lamenting desolately.

She saw a shadow moving by the water. It would be Birkin. . . .

From "The Snake," one of Lawrence's finest animal poems, written while he was living at Taormina in Sicily:

A snake came to my water-trough
On a hot, hot day, and I in pyjamas for the heat,
To drink there.

In the deep, strange-scented shade of the great
    dark carob tree
I came down the steps with my pitcher
And must wait, must stand and wait, for there he
    was at the trough before me.

He reached down from a fissure in the earth-wall
    in the gloom
And trailed his yellow-brown slackness soft-
    bellied down,
    Over the edge of the stone trough
And rested his throat upon the stone bottom,
And where the water had dripped from the tap,
    in a small clearness,
He sipped with his straight mouth,
Softly drank through his straight gums, into his
    slack long body,
Silently.

Someone was before me at my water-trough,
And I, like a second-comer, waiting

He lifted his head from his drinking, as cattle do,
And looked at me vaguely, as cattle do,
And flickered his two-forked tongue from his
   lips, and mused a moment,
And stooped and drank a little more,
Being earth-brown, earth-golden from the burn-
   ing bowels of the earth
On the day of Sicilian July, with Etna smoking. . . .

Lawrence's Chief Works

The White Peacock (1911)[†]
Sons and Lovers (1913)[*†]
The Rainbow (1915)[†]
Look! We Have Come Through (poems) (1913)
Twilight in Italy (1916)[*†]
Women in Love (1920)[*†]
The Prussian Officer, and Other Stories (1914)[*†]
Aaron's Rod (1922)[†]
Birds, Beasts and Flowers (poems) (1923)[*†]
Kangaroo (1924)[†]
The Plumed Serpent (1926)[†]
Mornings in Mexico (1927)[†]

[*]major works
[†]mentioned in text

The Woman Who Rode Away, and Other Stories
(1928)
Lady Chatterley's Lover (1928)*†
Pansies (poems) (1929)
Nettles (poems) (1930)
Love Among the Haystacks, and Other Pieces
(1930)
Apocalypse (1931)†
Last Poems (1932)*†
Etruscan Places (1932)*†

Chronology of Lawrence's Life and Times

1885	David Herbert Lawrence born June 11, at Eastwood, Nottinghamshire, in England.
1888	Jack the Ripper murders in East End of London.
1895	Trial of Oscar Wilde.
1898	Lawrence wins scholarship to Nottingham High School.
1899	Freud publishes *The Interpretation of Dreams*.
1899–1902	British fight Boer War in South Africa.

1901	Lawrence first meets Jessie Chambers.
1902	Becomes student-teacher at local Eastwood school for miners' children.
1903	First powered flight by Wright brothers in America.
1905	Einstein publishes first paper on relativity.
1906	Lawrence's first poems published.
1907	Picasso paints *Les Demoiselles d'Avignon*, instigating break with classical art and advent of cubism.
1912	Lawrence's tuberculosis forces him to abandon teaching career. Meets Frieda von Richthofen Weekley, and elopes with her to Europe. Finishes *Sons and Lovers* (published 1913).
1914	Lawrence and Frieda married in London. Outbreak of World War I.
1915	Lawrence's friendship with Bertrand Russell.

1916	Moves to Cornwall. Breaks with Russell. Writes *Women in Love* (published 1920).
1917	Outbreak of Russian Revolution in St. Petersburg.
1918	End of World War I.
1919	Versailles Peace Conference outside Paris attended by leaders of victorious allies: Woodrow Wilson, David Lloyd George, and Georges Clemenceau. Lawrence leaves England for Italy—the beginning of his years of self-imposed exile.
1921	Writes *Sea and Sardinia*.
1922	Annus mirabilis of modern literature: James Joyce publishes *Ulysses*; T. S. Eliot publishes *The Waste Land*; Rainer Maria Rilke completes *Duino Elegies*. Lawrence leaves Europe, travels to Ceylon (Sri Lanka). Settles briefly in Australia and writes *Kangaroo*. Finally reaches America and settles

	at Taos, New Mexico. *Fantasia of the Unconscious* published.
1923	Publication of *Birds, Beasts and Flowers* (poems).
1924	Begins *Mornings in Mexico*.
1926	May: general strike brings Britain to a halt. Lawrence's last visit to England. Publication of *The Plumed Serpent*. Begins writing *Lady Chatterley's Lover*. Lawrence's final return to Europe.
1927	Charles Lindbergh makes first solo flight across the Atlantic in his monoplane *Spirit of St. Louis*.
1929	Wall Street crash precipitates worldwide Great Depression. Lawrence writes *Apocalypse*.
1930	Lawrence dies in Vence in the South of France.

Recommended Reading

Richard Aldington, *D. H. Lawrence: Portrait of a Genius, But—* (Simon and Schuster, 1961). An unbuttoned portrait of Lawrence by his close but later somewhat disillusioned fellow writer and friend. Like many of the works of its subject, this caused a great scandal when it first appeared.

Frank Kermode, *D. H. Lawrence* (Viking, 1973). A short but deeply insightful book in the Modern Masters series by one of Britain's leading literary critics. Not cluttered with modern critical theory and its deadening jargon, this tells it as it is.

D. H. Lawrence, *Selected Letters*, edited by Richard Aldington (Penguin, 1996). Lawrence was an avid and persistent correspondent, and his letters contain pieces of his finest writing. Here he describes his travels and the people he meets with his un-mistakable eye for weakness, strength, detail, and atmosphere. He also, of course, expresses his opinions and ideas on just about everything. This is the informal Lawrence, where he is both at his most endearing and his most infuriating.

F. R. Leavis, *D. H. Lawrence: Novelist* (Vintage, 1975). The detailed study of Lawrence's greatest novels by his most sympathetic critic. Leavis was the first to place Lawrence in the canon of great twentieth-century writers, and for this we are in his debt. Leavis's writing was to advocate an en-tirely fresh way of looking at literature and in-spire a generation of readers.

Jeffrey Meyers, *D. H. Lawrence: A Biography* (Cooper Square, 2002). There are innumerable biographies of Lawrence; this is probably the most readable and balanced. It tells the story of Lawrence's ever-fascinating life in thoroughgoing fashion. It is up to date and includes much in-triguing detail without swamping the reader with unnecessary facts.

Harry T. Moore, *D. H. Lawrence and His World* (Viking, 1966). A picture can often be worth pages of words. This copiously illustrated book contains photos from every period of Lawrence's life, including most of the important people he met and the places he lived. The text provides a more than adequate commentary.

Frieda Lawrence von Richthofen, *Not I, But the Wind* (Scholarly Press, 1972). The very revealing and in many ways deeply moving memoir by Frieda of her life with Lawrence and their travels through four continents. The book is both petty and inspiring. She was, after all, the only other person who was there with him for most of the time.

Michael Squires and Lynn K. Talbot, *Living at the Edge: A Biography of D. H. Lawrence and Frieda von Richthofen* (University of Wisconsin Press, 2002). An intriguing "double biography" which succeeds in bringing Frieda out of the shadows, showing her effect on Lawrence's work and on his life. It also has some interesting insight into Lawrence and the people he and Frieda encountered on their travels around the world.

Index

A NOTE ON THE AUTHOR

Paul Strathern has lectured in philosophy and mathematics and now lives and writes in London. He is the author of the enormously successful series Philosophers in 90 Minutes. A Somerset Maugham Prize winner, he is also the author of books on history and travel, as well as five novels. His articles have appeared in a great many publications, including the *Observer* (London) and the *Irish Times*.

Paul Strathern's 90 Minutes series in philosophy, also published by Ivan R. Dee, includes individual books on Thomas Aquinas, Aristotle, St. Augustine, Berkeley, Confucius, Derrida, Descartes, Dewey, Foucault, Hegel, Heidegger, Hume, Kant, Kierkegaard, Leibniz, Locke, Machiavelli, Marx, J. S. Mill, Nietzsche, Plato, Rousseau, Bertrand Russell, Sartre, Schopenhauer, Socrates, Spinoza, and Wittgenstein.